THE CHILDREN'S DIVORCE-SURVIVAL BOOK

DON'T FALL APART ON SATURDAYS!

WRITTEN BY ADOLPH MOSER Ed.D.

ILLUSTRATED BY DAVID MELTON

LANDMARK EDITIONS, INC.
1904 Foxridge Drive • Kansas City, KS 66106 • www.landmarkeditions.com

Third Printing

TEXT COPYRIGHT © 2000 BY ADOLPH J. MOSER
ILLUSTRATIONS COPYRIGHT © 2000 BY DAVID MELTON

International Standard Book Number: 0-933849-77-X (LIB.BDG.)

Library of Congress Cataloging-in-Publication Data
Moser, Adolph, J., 1938-
    Don't fall apart on Saturdays!:
    the children's divorce-survival book /
    written by Adolph J. Moser : illustrated by David Melton
    p. cm.
    Summary: Explores the problems experienced when parents divorce, suggesting ways to
handle such situations effectively.
ISBN 0-933849-77-X (alk. paper)
    1. Children of divorced parents-Juvenile literature.
    2. Divorced parents-Juvenile literature.
    3. Divorce-Juvenile literature.
    [1. Divorce.]

I. Melton, David, ill. II. Title
HQ777.5.M68   2000
306.874-dc21   00-027021

CIP

Editorial Coordinator: Nancy R. Thatch
Creative Coordinator: David Melton
Computer Graphics Coordinator: Gary C. Brees
Printed in the United States of America

Landmark Editions, Inc.
1904 Foxridge Drive
Kansas City, Kansas 66106
913-722-0700
www.landmarkeditions.com

Dear Friend:

If your parents decide to get a divorce, it can be very upsetting to you.

The purpose of this book is to ease many of your concerns and help you:

HOLD YOURSELF TOGETHER.

After you read this book yourself, I urge you to read it with your parents — one parent at a time. That will give you opportunities to ask them questions and discuss the things that bother you. Together, you and your parents can gain a better understanding of each other's feelings and solve many problems.

It is important for you to remember — Although your parents may no longer want to be married to each other, they still love you. And you love them.

I hope this book will be very helpful to you.

— Your Friend,
Adolph Moser

It happens every day—

Someone's parents
decide to get a divorce.

Hearing that their parents
are going to get a divorce
can be very upsetting
for the children.

"What is going to
become of our family?"
they wonder.
"Why is this happening to us?"

"Is it my fault?"
they worry.

"Did I do something
to make my parents
want to get a divorce?"
they ask.

NO!
is the answer.

It is NOT
the children's fault.
They have not done anything
to make their parents
want to get a divorce.

If your parents
decide to get a divorce,
it will NOT
be your fault either.

So —

DON'T BLAME YOURSELF!

You are not the reason
your parents married each other.
And you are not the reason
they decided to get a divorce.

The problem is not you.
The real problem
is between your parents.

Blaming yourself
is a very bad idea
and a waste of time.

Certificate of Marriage

It is officially certified
that from this day forward
this man and this woman
are legally married
and are hereby declared to be
husband and wife.

What is a marriage?
A marriage is
a legal document
between two people.

When two people marry,
they sign an agreement
that legally makes them
a Husband and a Wife.

When two people sign
a divorce agreement,
they are no longer married.

They become legally
single people again.
They become
an Ex-Husband
and an Ex-Wife.

"When my parents
get divorced,
will they also become
an Ex-Father and
an Ex-Mother?"
you may wonder.

NO!

Being divorced
does NOT change your
parents' relationships with you.

Your mother will still
legally be your mother.
And your father will still
legally be your father.

The love that parents
feel for their children
is different from the love
adults feel for one another.

Your parents'
feelings toward you
should not change
in any way.

"But what will my friends think
about the divorce?" you may ask.

Most of your friends
will be sorry
to hear about it.

18

Many of your friends
have had divorces
in their families,
so they will
understand that
you may feel upset.

"Will my parents still be mad
at each other after the divorce?"

Some parents stay mad
at each other
for a long time.

But other parents
become friendlier
and much nicer
to each other after
they are divorced.

After the divorce,
your parents may still
get angry and
say mean things
to each other.

Tell them they
are upsetting you
and ask them to please
try to be more pleasant
with one another.

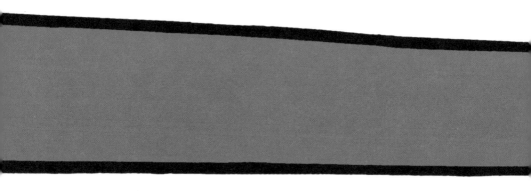

Some fathers tell
their children that
the divorce was
ALL their mother's fault.
And some mothers say
the fathers are to blame
for everything.

Usually, neither statement
is completely true.

Most often,
the divorce was
the fault of
BOTH of the parents.

If one of your parents
wants you to take
an unkind message
to the other parent,
say you would rather not
because you don't want to help
make the other parent angry.

If one of your parents
asks you to spy
on the other parent,
DON'T DO IT!

If the other parent
finds out that you are spying,
he or she won't like it.

When your parents argue
with one another,
you should try NOT
to take either side.

Let them settle
their own differences
without you getting
in the middle.

Your parents are not perfect.
Sometimes they make mistakes.

Although you love
your parents,
there may be times
when you will
really dislike them.

Don't let this upset you,
because feeling that way
is not unusual.
Most children dislike
their parents at times.

Hopefully,
you will have
more reasons
to like your parents
than to dislike them.

DIVORCE can be
a very scary experience
for everyone —
for children and
for Moms and Dads, too.

There are so many changes
happening all at once.
This can make
everyone feel nervous
and even frightened.

MOM'S HOUSE

After the divorce,
your parents won't live
in the same house anymore.

Sometimes,
you may live with your mom,
and sometimes,
you may live with your dad.

34

"Can't I say
where I want to live?"
you may ask.

Some children get to decide
which parent they live with.
But most often,
parents make that decision.

Some children
don't like to move
from one house
to the other.

But some children think
it's exciting and fun
to change back and forth
from Mom's house to Dad's house.

Whenever you are
with one of your parents,
you may miss the other one.
When you have this feeling,
phone your other parent,
or write a letter,
or send an e-mail.

It is important that
you tell your parents
how you feel and
what you are thinking.

If you have
trouble talking
to your parents
and explaining
your feelings to them,

then talk with
someone else —
such as a grandparent,
or a friend, or a teacher,
or a school counselor.

It may help you
if you talk with
other children whose
parents are divorced.

Or, if there is
a self-help group
at your school
or in your neighborhood,
you might want to join it.

Most children have
what is sometimes called
"THE GREAT HOPE".

They hope that
their mom and dad
will change their minds
and get back together again.

But that rarely happens.

Most divorced parents
do get married again,
but not to each other.
Instead,
most of them
marry other people.

When Dad and Mom
start dating other people,
the children often
start to worry.

"Are my parents
dating nice people?"
they wonder.

"Will these people like me?"
they ask.

Most often,
the people their parents date
are really nice.
The children like them,
and they like the children.

When your parents divorce,
it may be difficult
for you
to get used
to all of the changes.

But you will have to
face those changes,
day by day,
and try to keep yourself
from getting upset
      and
FALLING APART.

Saturdays can be very difficult
because there are often
more changes on Saturdays.
For instance:
Dad is supposed to pick up
you and your sister
and take you to his house
and then to the zoo.

You get everything packed
and you are ready on time,
because you know
Dad does not like
to be kept waiting.

50

DAYS!

But this morning — *Dad is late!*
You phone him, but get no answer.
Mom is nervous because
she plans to go shopping.
Your little sister begins to cry.
"Daddy isn't coming!" she says.

The phone rings — It's Dad.
"I'll be there in ten minutes,"
 he promises.
But thirty minutes pass.
Now Mom is pacing back and forth.
Everyone is upset and...
"Oh, no! It's starting to rain!"

To help you keep yourself
from FALLING APART,
draw a picture of yourself
on a piece of paper.

*No, you don't have
to be a great artist.*

Just draw a simple picture.

Your head is connected
to your neck.
Your neck is connected
to your chest.
Your hands are connected
to your arms.
Your arms and legs
are connected to your body.

You get the idea.

53

When you finish
your picture,
look at it carefully.

Label your arms and legs
as your emotional parts —

MY THOUGHTS

MY FEELINGS

MY HOPES

and

MY DREAMS

Now, your job is to try
to keep ALL
of your emotional parts
together.

DON'T FALL APART
ON SATURDAYS!

So, on the bottom
of your picture,
write the words —

DON'T FALL APART
ON SATURDAYS!

Put your picture on a wall
where you can see it.

When things upset you
ON SATURDAYS,

look at the picture
and read the message.

Take a deep breath
and RELAX!

If you can

keep yourself from

FALLING APART ON SATURDAYS,

then you can keep yourself

TOGETHER ON SUNDAYS,

and

ON MONDAYS,

and

ON ALL THE OTHER

DAYS OF THE WEEK.

59

Remember —
Your parents' divorce
is the end
of their marriage.
But it is NOT the end
of your relationships
with your parents.

For you,
it is the beginning
of new experiences
that you can enjoy
with each of
your parents.

SEVEN BOOKS! SEVEN DAYS!

STRESS!

ISBN 0-933849-18-4

SELF-ESTEEM!

ISBN 0-933849-38-9

ANGER!

ISBN 0-933849-54-0

GRIEF!

ISBN 0-933849-60-5

TRUTH!

ISBN 0-933849-76-1

DIVORCE!

ISBN 0-933849-77-X

VIOLENCE!

ISBN 0-933849-79-6

ALL SEVEN ARE IMPORTANT BOOKS!

In these very informative and highly entertaining handbooks for children, Dr. Adolph Moser offers practical approaches and effective techniques to help youngsters deal with the problems of –

STRESS, SELF-ESTEEM, ANGER, GRIEF, TRUTH, DIVORCE, and *VIOLENCE.*

The colorful illustrations created by artists Dav Pilkey and David Melton project perfect blends of humor and sensitivity.

YOU'LL WANT ALL OF THEM!

EMOTIONAL IMPACT SERIES

Children love these books because they help children deal with real problems that they face every day.

Counselors, teachers, and parents appreciate the practical advice these books offer to the youngsters who are in their care.

These Outstanding Books Are Highly Recommended

Much-needed books!
I enthusiastically recommend all of them to parents, teachers, clinicians, and, of course, to children.
— Theodore Tollefson, Ph.D. Clinical Psychologist

Delightful and practical!
You don't have to be a psychologist to read these books to a child.
Better still, have a child read them to you.
— Larry M. Hubble, Ph.D. Psychologist

What helpful books for teaching children important methods of self-control. I highly recommend them!
— Suzanne Leiphant, Ph.D. Clinical Psychologist & Author

Informative, compassionate, wise!
These helpful handbooks clearly explain and entertain at the same time.
— Dr. Taylor McGee, HSPP Child Psychologist

One only has to read today's headlines or hear the news to realize how much these books are needed.
— Phyllis Morrison Grateful Parent

These are very important books.
I have no doubt they could help save the lives of many children and adults, too.
— R.M. Fortrell, Ph.D. Psychologist

Adolph Moser — author

Dr. Adolph Moser is a licensed clinical psychologist in private practice, specializing in bio-behavioral and cognitive approaches to stress-related syndromes. He is founder of the Center for Human Potential, a nonprofit organization with holistic focus on preventing acute onsets of stress in children. While Chief Psychologist at the Indiana Youth Center, he implemented a biofeedback laboratory and directed a nine-year research project on the effects of relaxation techniques in the treatment of stress disorders. That study culminated in the development of the nationally distributed stress-management program, entitled SYSTEMATIC RELAXATION TRAINING.

Raised in Indiana, Dr. Moser is a graduate of the universities of Purdue and Indiana. He is certified in biofeedback and is a Diplomate Stressologist. He is also a Diplomate in Behavioral Medicine and Psychotherapy, and a Fellow and Diplomate in Medical Psychotherapy. Dr. Moser is listed in WHO'S WHO IN THE BIO-BEHAVIORAL SCIENCES. In 1987, he received the "Outstanding Psychologist of the Year" award from the National Prisoners' Rights Union.

After becoming parents, Dr. Moser and his wife, Dr. Kathryn Moser, who is also a psychologist, expanded their professional practices to include normal problems of childhood and parenting. They co-authored a newspaper column, "Positive Parenting," for ten years.

Dr. Moser is the father of three children, spanning pre-school to adolescence, which explains his perennial interest in stress and anger management.

All of Dr. Moser's books in his EMOTIONAL IMPACT SERIES have received outstanding reviews and enthusiastic acceptance from children, parents, counselors, and educators nationwide.

David Melton — illustrator

David Melton is one of the most versatile and prolific talents on the literary and art scenes today. His literary works span the gamut of factual prose, news-reporting, analytical essays, magazine articles, features, short stories, and poetry and novels in both the adult and juvenile fields. In the past thirty years, twenty-one of his books have been published. Several of them have been translated into a number of foreign languages.

Mr. Melton has illustrated ten of his own books and seven by other authors. Many of his drawings and paintings have been reproduced as fine art prints, posters, puzzles, calendars, book jackets, record covers, mobiles, and note cards, and have been featured in national publications.

Since a number of Mr. Melton's books are enjoyed by children, he has visited hundreds of schools throughout the country as a principal speaker in Young Authors' Days, Author-in-Residence Programs, and Children's Literature Festivals. Each year, he also conducts his WRITTEN & ILLUSTRATED BY... WORKSHOPS for students and educators, effectively teaching participants to write and illustrate original books.

Mr. Melton's teacher's manual, WRITTEN & ILLUSTRATED BY..., has been highly acclaimed and has been used by thousands of teachers nationwide to instruct their students in how to write and illustrate amazing books.

Mr. Melton is also a book publisher. During the last fourteen years, as Creative Coordinator at Landmark Editions, he has supervised the publication of more than fifty books by other authors and illustrators.